Disney's WORLD OF ADVENTURE

CARS!

presents

CARS! CARS!

Random House 🏠 New York

Photograph Credits: A. Devaney, Inc., 48 bottom; Gero Hoschek/Alpha Photos, 44, 45 top, 46; Danilo Nardi/Freelance Photographer Guild Inc., 48 top; Ed Radlauer, 49, 50, 51, 52, 53; Al Satterwaite/Camera 5, 47 both; John Zimmerman/Freelance Photographer Guild Inc., 45 bottom.

Copyright © 1977 by Walt Disney Productions. All rights reserved under International and Pan-American Copyright Conventions. Published in the United States by Random House, Inc., New York, and simultaneously in Canada by Random House of Canada Limited, Toronto.

Library of Congress Cataloging in Publication Data

Disney (Walt) Productions. Disney's world of adventure presents Cars! Cars! Cars! contents: The love bug.—How to make a love-bug-mobile.—U.S. auto races.—In other words.—Soap box derby.—Goofy enters the soap box derby. 1. Automobiles—Design and construction—Juvenile literature. 2. Automobile racing—Juvenile literature. 3. Soap box derbies—Juvenile literature. [1. Automobiles, Racing—Fiction. 2. Soap box derbies—Fiction. 3. Automobiles—Design and construction. 4. Automobile racing. 5. Soap box derbies] I. Title. PZ7.D625Car 790.19′22 77-74465 ISBN 0-394-83598-0 ISBN 0-394-93598-5 lib. bdg.

Manufactured in the United States of America 1 2 3 4 5 6 7 8 9 0

Contents

The Love Bug	8
How to Make a Love-Bug-Mobile	35
In Other Words	42
U.S. Auto Races	44
Soap Box Derby	49
Goofy Enters The Soap Box Derby	54

The Love Bug

An Unwilling Customer

HERBIE WAS a plain, small car. He looked exactly like all the other plain, small cars that came from the factory that year. At first no one noticed that he was special.

Jim Douglas would never have noticed. He rarely even looked at plain, small cars. Jim was a race car driver. He liked fancy cars with big, powerful engines.

On the day this story begins, Jim was standing in a sports car show-

room. He was surrounded by fancy cars. In the middle of the room, a shiny yellow Lotus 500 caught his eye. With a car like that, he thought, I could start winning races again.

"May I help you, sir?" said a tall man with a well-trimmed mustache. He was wearing a red carnation on his suit. "I am Mr. Thorndyke, the owner of this fine showroom. You look like a man who wishes to buy a fine car."

Jim smiled. He knew that he couldn't even afford to buy a used jalopy.

"That's my *wish*," he said. "But—"

"Good!" cried Mr. Thorndyke. "I love to sell a car . . . I mean, I love to make a wish come true. Allow me to pour you some sherry."

He reached over and pressed a button. The top of a tall cabinet opened up. Mr. Thorndyke took out a bottle and poured some sherry into a small glass.

"How much would you like to spend?" asked Mr. Thorndyke, handing the glass to Jim. "Ten thousand? Twenty thousand? Thirty thousand?"

"Seventy-five dollars would be about right," said Jim.

Mr. Thorndyke snatched the glass out of his hand.

"In that case," Mr. Thorndyke said, pouring Jim's sherry back in the bottle, "I will bid you good day."

Suddenly something bumped into Jim.

"Hey!" he cried.

Mr. Thorndyke looked up from the sherry bottle. There behind Jim stood a plain, small white car.

Of course, it was a perfectly nice little automobile. But it did look rather odd parked in Mr. Thorndyke's showroom. All of the other cars were long and low and very sleek. The small white car was

10

short and bulgy and shaped like a bug.

"Havershaw!" shouted Mr. Thorndyke. "What is this *thing* doing in my showroom?"

A short man wearing big round glasses came out of the office.

"What thing, sir?" he asked.

"This clown buggy!" said Mr. Thorndyke, pointing at the small white car.

"Oh, that, sir?" said Havershaw. "You remember when Mrs. Van de Riche bought the Porsche for her son, she asked us to find a little car for her maid. It was returned today. The maid said she was having trouble with it."

"I don't want to hear what the maid said," snapped Mr. Thorndyke. "I just want to know—what is it doing *here*?"

"It doesn't seem to be doing anything, sir," said Havershaw.

"Of course not, you thimblewit!" cried Mr. Thorndyke. "What do you expect it to do—roll out of the showroom by itself? Now get rid of this doodlebug before I lose my temper!" And he kicked the small car as hard as he could.

"Hey, why don't you leave the little car alone?" said Jim.

Mr. Thorndyke glared at him.

"Are you trying to tell me how to act in my own showroom?" he said. "I thought I bid you good day."

Jim shrugged and headed out. As he was leaving through the front door, Havershaw was pushing the small car out the back.

Five minutes later, Jim got on a bus to go home. At that moment a small white car rolled out of the alley next to the showroom. The car was empty. No one was driving it.

As the bus pulled away from the curb, the little car zipped up behind it and followed it down the street.

Jim lived with his friend Tennessee, a sculptor. Their home had once been a fire station.

The next morning Jim was upstairs in the kitchen staring gloomily into the refrigerator. The hissing sound of a blowtorch was coming from below.

"Alfalfa seeds! Soy nuts! Wheat germ!" Jim grumbled as he read the labels on the jars in the refrigerator. "How is anyone supposed to get a decent breakfast around here?"

He closed the refrigerator door and went downstairs.

The ground floor was Tennessee's workshop. Once, fire engines had been kept there. Now it was piled around the sides with pieces of wrecked cars—smashed doors, dented fenders, busted cables. In the center of the room there was another pile. This pile reached to the ceiling. It was made of old car parts welded together. Exhaust pipes, rusty gears, and broken axles stuck out in all directions.

"Hey, Tennessee!" called Jim. "Can I use your car today? There's a race at the fairgrounds."

A fat, pudgy-faced man stepped out from behind the tower of welded metal. He wore baggy pants and a baggy sweatshirt. One hand held a blowtorch.

"Sure," said Tennessee, walking over to Jim. "But you may have trouble getting it started."

He pointed to the center of the room. There, at the top of the tower, was the chromium nameplate from a 1959 Edsel.

"Oh, no! You didn't cut up the old beast?" cried Jim.

"It came over me suddenly," said Tennessee. "I think my car will be a lot happier as a piece of art."

Jim went back up the stairs. Tennessee followed him into the kitchen.

"That car was my last hope," said Jim. "I can't even borrow a car anymore. I've lost so many races, no one wants to take a chance on me."

Tennessee sat down at the table.

"Maybe you should try doing something else," he said. "Look at me. I wasn't always a metal sculptor. I used to paint flower seeds. I thought I was happy. Then, one day, I heard a little voice inside me say, 'Tennessee?' I said, 'What?' The voice said, 'You are not happy.'"

Jim opened the refrigerator door and stood staring at the jars of nuts and seeds.

"Well, the next day I got on a boat and went to Tibet," Tennessee went on. "Soon I was up on a mountaintop with the gurus and the swamis. I was sitting with my legs crossed, looking at my stomach. I was sipping a little herb tea. I began to see things as they really are. I discovered my real self. It was wonderful!"

"Tell me something, Tennessee," said Jim. "Why do we have all this parrot food in the house? We don't *have* a parrot."

Just then they heard a voice calling from outside. Jim and Tennessee went over to the window and leaned out.

A policeman was standing below. Behind him, parked in their driveway, was a small white car.

"Good morning!" called the policeman. "Have you ever seen this car before?"

"It's a cute little car," said Tennessee. "But it doesn't live here."

"Hey, wait a minute!" said Jim. "I think I saw that car in a showroom yesterday."

"Then would you mind coming with me?" said the policeman.

"What for?" asked Jim.

"Have you ever heard of a thing called grand larceny?" asked the policeman.

"But I didn't steal it," cried Jim "I have no idea how that little car got here."

"You can explain that to the owner," said the policeman. "Shall we go?"

Jim left the window and went downstairs. Tennessee was still looking at the small car. Suddenly it jumped! It was just a little jump, but Tennessee was sure he saw all four wheels leave the ground.

As Jim and the policeman were hitching the small car to the police tow truck, Tennessee came out of the firehouse.

"I'm coming with you, Jim," he said. "I think you're going to need my help."

When they pulled into the alley next to the showroom, they saw a dark-haired young woman in coveralls. She was leaning over the engine of a fancy red race car. She looked up, slid off the fender, and walked over to the men.

"Hi!" she said. "I'm Carole Bennett, Mr. Thorndyke's mechanic. I see you found the missing car."

"It was parked in this guy's driveway," said the policeman, pointing at Jim.

"You don't look like a car thief," said Carole.

"I'm not," said Jim. "There's been a mistake."

"Then I'm sure everything can be straightened out very quickly," she said. "Here's Mr. Thorndyke now."

Mr. Thorndyke stepped out the back door of the showroom. He was wearing a very fancy outfit—red jumpsuit, red helmet, red gloves. A pair of black goggles was perched on his forehead. He joined the group standing beside the little car.

"Ah, good morning, Officer," said Mr. Thorndyke. "I see you found the culprit. He was here yesterday. Lock him up. We can't have car thieves on the loose, can we?"

"Then you'll have to come down to headquarters with us, Mr. Thorndyke," said the policeman.

"That is impossible," said Mr. Thorndyke. "I'm driving in a race at the fairgrounds today. Miss Bennett and I were just about to leave."

"Say, Jim," said Tennessee. "Why don't you buy the little car? I think it likes you."

"I don't want this car," said Jim. "And even if I did, I don't have enough money to buy it."

Mr. Thorndyke glanced at his watch.

"I am not in the habit of selling cars to bums," said Mr. Thorndyke.

"Now wait a minute!" Jim cried angrily.

"BUT," Mr. Thorndyke went on, "I am in a hurry. So I will give you the chance to buy the car. Give Havershaw a small down payment and the car is yours. You can owe us the rest of the money—with interest, of course."

"I think Mr. Thorndyke is being very fair," said the policeman.

"Look at it this way, Jim," said Tennessee. "You need a car. This car needs a good home."

"Okay, I'll buy it," said Jim wearily. "I've seen a lot of crummy stunts to sell cars. But this beats them all!"

"How dare you insult me!" said Mr. Thorndyke. "I would be most happy to see you thrown in jail and that dumb-looking car dropped into the bay."

Suddenly Mr. Thorndyke heard the sound of something squirting. He looked down. A fountain of black, sticky oil was shooting out from under the small white car. It was splattering all over Mr. Thorndyke's fancy red racing costume.

Off to the Races

As Jim and Tennessee drove away from the showroom, Jim said, "Tennessee, you were no help at all. Whose side were you on, anyway?"

"I guess I was on Herbie's side," said Tennessee.

"Herbie?" said Jim. "Who is Herbie?"

"That's what I named your new car," answered Tennessee.

"Why on earth did you do that?"

"Well, it's this way," said Tennessee slowly. "Horace didn't seem to fit. Mortimer has too many syllables. Oogie seemed . . ."

"No, no, no," Jim said. "I meant, why did you give it a name? This car is just a machine."

"I give names to lots of machines," said Tennessee. "The washing machine is Clyde. The vending machine at the gas station is Bert. The gumball machine at the market is Harold. I look at it

this way. When the world is taken over by machines, at least I will know a few of them personally."

"That's crazy," said Jim. "Why do you think the world is going to be taken over by machines?"

"It's already starting to happen," said Tennessee. "We make machines. We stuff them with information. They get to be smarter than we are. One day these machines are going to be too smart. That's when they'll start to run things."

They drove past a long line of cars waiting to turn left.

"Where were all those cars going?" asked Tennessee, looking back.

"That was the turnoff to the fairgrounds," said Jim.

Suddenly the little car jolted to a stop. Jim glanced down. His foot was still on the gas pedal.

Before he could begin to wonder about this, something more unusual happened. The little car rose up a few inches off the road and spun around. After it landed, it zipped back to the intersection and turned right.

"Wow!" cried Tennessee. "Herbie is amazing!"

"There is nothing amazing about this car," said Jim as Herbie sped on down the road. "It just wants to go one way and I want to go another."

"Don't you think that's amazing?" asked Tennessee.

"Not at all," said Jim. "Some wires must be crossed. I'll pull over and have a look."

But when he pressed down on the brake, nothing happened.

Soon they were passing acres and acres of parked cars. As they neared the entrance to the fair, they saw mobs of people crowding in at the gates. Herbie swerved to the right. They went down a dirt road that circled the fairgrounds.

They traveled past the livestock exhibit, past the mobile-home show, past the ferris wheel. Then they came to the grandstand. Herbie

darted through an open gate. He charged up a ramp and down another. When he finally came to a stop, Jim and Tennessee found themselves sitting on the racetrack.

Straight ahead, twenty race cars were lined up in rows across the track. Suddenly the stillness was shattered by a powerful roar. It was the roar of twenty engines coming to life. Far beyond, a green flag flashed in the sunlight. The race cars took off, leaving Jim, Tennessee, and Herbie parked in a cloud of dust.

Then a kind of rumbling noise began. Herbie started to shake. The rumbling grew louder and louder. All at once, Herbie leaped forward and raced after the other cars.

Within seconds, he had caught up with the pack.

Jim gripped the steering wheel. Expertly, easily, he guided his car through one turn after another. He was calm—the way a race driver feels when he is doing everything right.

Lap after lap, Herbie kept up with the other cars. But he stayed in last place.

"Nice going, Herbie," said Tennessee. "Don't make it look too easy."

Just as Herbie entered the backstretch in the last lap, he seemed to let loose. Instantly Jim swung the car out from behind the pack. Herbie shot forward ahead of all the cars but one—a fancy red race car.

The driver in the lead car was not surprised to find himself far out in front. He knew that he had the fastest car on the track. But when he glanced in his rear-view mirror, he was positively flabbergasted. A small white car was right on his tail!

"Hey, it's Mr. Thorndyke!" Tennessee cried out. "Come on, Herbie!"

Herbie tried to pass the red car. But Thorndyke swung over and blocked the way.

"He's cutting us off!" yelled Tennessee. "He won't let us by!"

Thorndyke laughed wildly. Again and again he swerved to block the little white car.

Suddenly Jim and Tennessee found themselves staring up at the

sky. Herbie was rolling along on his back wheels. His front wheels were spinning high in the air.

Herbie looked ridiculous.

The people in the grandstand sprang out of their seats. They couldn't take their eyes off the small white car. And neither could Mr. Thorndyke! He was staring so hard into his rear-view mirror that he didn't see where he was going. He drove right off the track. His car crashed into a pile of hay—three feet from the finish line.

Herbie rolled on by. A split-second later, Jim had won the race.

Fuming, Mr. Thorndyke crawled out of his red race car. Hay was dangling from his mustache.

"I'll get even!" he shrieked.

Mr. Thorndyke was not a very good loser.

That evening Tennessee was downstairs in the firehouse with Herbie.

"There!" he said, stepping back and putting down his paintbrush. "Now you look like a real race car."

Herbie beeped.

He was wearing red and blue racing stripes and a number—53.

"Well, I'm back in action now," said Jim as he came down the stairs. "Four big races are coming up. I'm driving in all of them."

"Herbie will love that," said Tennessee.

"Yeah, I'm going to make that little car famous," said Jim. "I did everything right today. My driving has never been better."

"What about Herbie?" asked Tennessee. "Don't you think he deserves some credit, too?"

"I think you're a little mixed up about who won that race," said Jim. "This car is just a bunch of nuts and bolts. Sure, it's got more speed than you would expect. But I was the one doing the driving."

"Don't pay any attention to him, Herbie," said Tennessee, patting the little car's hood. "His head is all swelled up with importance. Winning does that to some people."

The Whipped Cream Disaster

Herbie did become famous in the next few months. He won every race that Jim entered. At Monterey he set a new record for finishing time. At Laguna Seca, he set a new record for lap speed. At the Las Vegas Open, he set another kind of record. He was the first car to take all the turns on one wheel.

Mr. Thorndyke began to have eye trouble. He kept seeing a small white car whiz by him.

The day after the Las Vegas Open, he was sitting in his office with Carole. She was looking at the morning newspaper.

"You don't look well in these pictures," said Carole.

"How could I look well?" cried Mr. Thorndyke. "I can't sleep. That rotten little car is driving me buggy!"

"Why do you keep blaming that car for all your defeats?" asked Carole. "Maybe Mr. Douglas is just a better driver."

"Balderdash!" said Mr. Thorndyke. "There isn't a driver in the world who can get that much speed out of a car like that."

"I think you are letting this whole thing get to you," said Carole. "Why don't you just forget about the little car?"

"Forget? Never!" cried Mr. Thorndyke. "It's just time to try a new strategy."

The night before the big race at Riverside, Tennessee was standing in his workshop gazing proudly at Herbie. He had been working on the little car all day—cleaning and polishing. There was nothing more he could do. Herbie was in perfect shape.

He was surprised to hear a knock at the firehouse door. When he opened it, he saw Mr. Thorndyke.

"Oh, hi," said Tennessee. "I hear you're driving in the race tomorrow. Did you come to see Jim? He's asleep."

"No, I came to see this fine little automobile," said Mr. Thorndyke, walking over to Herbie.

"Yes, he's a terrific car, all right," said Tennessee. "But I thought you might not like Herbie. He's been winning a lot of races."

Mr. Thorndyke laughed. "I can be a good sport, can't I?"

"Well, in that case, would you like some hot chocolate?" asked Tennessee. "I was just about to make some."

"That would be nice," said Mr. Thorndyke.

Tennessee went upstairs. Quickly, Mr. Thorndyke raised Herbie's front hood. For a moment he thought he had discovered the secret of the little car. It didn't have an engine! Then he remembered that the small car's engine was in back, not in front. Under the hood there was nothing but a big empty space and the gas cap.

Here's my chance to do something to this car, thought Mr. Thorndyke. Now what shall it be?

"How about some whipped cream?" Tennessee asked, coming back down the stairs. He was holding a tall can. "It goes well with hot chocolate."

"Whipped cream?" said Mr. Thorndyke. "Why, yes, that is just what I need."

"Good," said Tennessee. He set the can on a bench next to some cups. "I'll be right back with the hot chocolate."

"Don't hurry," called Mr. Thorndyke merrily as Tennessee disappeared.

He grabbed the can of whipped cream and twisted off Herbie's gas cap. Pfssht! Foaming cream squirted into the little car's gas tank.

Thorndyke was just closing Herbie's hood when he heard a strange hissing sound. He backed away from the car in alarm.

Tennessee came down the stairs. He was holding a blowtorch under a small pot. Sparks were flying.

"It heats faster this way," said Tennessee, nodding at the pot of hot chocolate.

"That's a clever trick," said Mr. Thorndyke. "Well, I really must be going. Toodle-oo!"

He walked out of the firehouse. Tennessee stood staring after him.

At the Riverside Raceway the next afternoon, the big race of the day had just begun. A pack of race cars roared past the grandstand. People were cheering. A voice came over the loudspeaker.

"The cars are spreading out now," said the announcer. "It looks as if Peter Thorndyke, in car number fourteen, has taken the lead. But here comes car number fifty-three, moving up quickly. The Douglas car is right behind car number fourteen. He's starting to pass! There he goes, folks! It looks as if Jim Douglas has this race well in control."

Jim settled back in his seat. He was now far out in front. Just then the little car coughed. Jim sat up tensely. Herbie was beginning to sputter. He was slowing down. The other cars sped by.

Jim pressed down on the gas pedal to make Herbie go faster. Herbie burped.

Just as the little car came into the far turn, it lurched. Herbie toppled head over heels—or rather, hood over wheels. He landed on the track upside down.

Then Herbie began to rock from side to side. He looked like a bug trying to turn itself over. At last, with a mighty jerk, he flipped up on his right side wheels. For several seconds he teetered back and forth. Then, with a final groan, Herbie plopped back down. His wheels stuck straight up in the air. A few gooey white bubbles came out of his exhaust pipe.

Jim pushed open the door and wiggled out of the car, head first. Without giving Herbie another glance, he walked off the track and disappeared.

As Herbie was being towed from the track, the announcer's voice came over the loudspeaker.

"It's car number fourteen, crossing the finish line! Peter Thorndyke has won this race."

The tow truck, with Herbie hitched to it, wound its way slowly through the pit area. As it came to a crowd of people, it stopped. Not far away, a ring of reporters and photographers was gathered around Mr. Thorndyke.

"Ladies and gentlemen," said Mr. Thorndyke as he posed to have his picture taken. "I think we have seen the last of Jim Douglas and his trick car."

Just then Mr. Thorndyke heard a burping sound. He glanced at Herbie. Something wet and foamy landed on his face. It was a glob of whipped cream.

That evening Tennessee was standing in the firehouse driveway looking sadly at Herbie's engine. It was covered with gooey white bubbles.

"Poor little fellow!" he said. "Who could have done this to you?"

He stuck his finger in the white goo and tasted it. It was sweet, like whipped cream.

"Thorndyke!" cried Tennessee. "I should never have left him alone with you, Herbie. But don't you worry. Jim will be here soon. He must have had something very important to do."

"Hi!" said a familiar voice. Tennessee looked up and saw Carole Bennett.

"I just came over to tell Jim that I'm not working for Mr. Thorndyke anymore," she said. "I found

out what he did to Jim's car."

"I knew you would be on our side," said Tennessee. "But Jim's not here. He disappeared right after Herbie had his accident."

"Doesn't he take care of his car after a race?" asked Carole.

"You're a mechanic," said Tennessee. "Can you do something for the little car? He seems to be suffering."

"Suffering?" said Carole.

"Yeah, Herbie isn't like other cars," said Tennessee. "He runs on love. Right now, he needs a lot of love and attention. Jim doesn't understand Herbie. He would be here if he did."

Carole went to work on the little car. Tennessee began telling her all about Herbie.

An hour later, Carole closed Herbie's hood.

"The little car is in fine shape now," she said. "The fuel lines are clean. The plugs are clean. The wiring checks out."

"Herbie and I want to thank you," said Tennessee.

The little car made a happy whirring sound.

"You know," said Carole, "I think I'm beginning to believe what you say about this car."

Just then Jim drove up behind Herbie in a fancy green sports car. Herbie made a low, rumbling sound.

"Hi!" said Jim. "How do you like my new car?"

"You already have a car," said Tennessee. "Herbie is your car."

"I'm not going to be driving Herbie anymore," said Jim. "The road race at El Dorado is coming up next week. I need a strong, powerful car—something I can believe in."

"What's going to happen to Herbie?" asked Tennessee.

"I'll sell him," said Jim. "I could use the money."

Herbie whined softly.

"Let's go inside so Herbie won't hear you talking this way," said Tennessee. "Can't you see he's jealous of your new car?"

As they went into the firehouse, Jim said, "Will you stop acting as if Herbie can hear and see and think and feel? He's just a car. Tell him, Carole."

"No, I'll tell you something," she said, turning to Jim. "I think Herbie *is* special. His engine is very ordinary. Yet he does extraordinary things. He's won a lot of races for you. He's been your best friend. You can't sell him! That would be a rotten thing to do."

"It wasn't Herbie's fault that he turned upside down today," said Tennessee. "Mr. Thorndyke poured a can of whipped cream into his gas tank last night. Herbie tried, but he just couldn't keep going on a tankful of whipped cream. The poor little car had a tummyache."

Suddenly they heard a loud crash. It came from the driveway.

Jim ran outside. His new car was sitting in the street. Its front end was smashed. Herbie was banging up against it.

Jim grabbed a wrench.

"No!" he cried, rushing at Herbie.

"Stop, Jim!" called Tennessee, coming up from behind. "You don't know what you're doing!"

Jim dropped the wrench. He stood staring in amazement as the little car rolled away down the street.

"Herbie! Herbie!" cried Jim, running after him. "Come back!"

Herbie Strikes Back

Late that night, a small white car wove its way slowly through the city. Every now and then it made a sad little whirring sound. Once it bumped into a trash can. At last, it rolled up onto a sidewalk and came to rest in front of a large window.

The little car had run out of gas—right in front of Mr. Thorndyke's showroom.

Thorndyke! The man who played dirty tricks on innocent little

cars! Herbie began to rumble. He was shaking all over. All of a sudden, he lunged forward and crashed through the showroom window.

When Jim stepped through that window an hour later, he found Herbie parked in a pile of broken glass.

Mr. Thorndyke was rushing around wildly, shouting orders at Havershaw.

"Call the police! Call the insurance company! Call the tow truck! Call the glass factory!"

Havershaw was rushing around, too, trying to decide which thing to do first.

"I'm here, Herbie," said Jim. "Everything is going to be all right now."

Herbie beeped softly.

"Aha!" Mr. Thorndyke cried, seeing Jim. "You owe me a thousand dollars for the broken window."

"I don't have a thousand dollars," said Jim.

"Then give me the little car," said Thorndyke. "I just happen to know a nice auto wrecking company. They have the most wonderful claw and hook. I can see it now. Up goes the little car—high into the air. Bang! It drops into that lovely compressing machine. Ah, those crunching sounds! How I will love hearing them! Then out comes the little car—crushed into a box of metal."

"I won't give you Herbie," said Jim. "I'll pay you for the window after the road race at El Dorado. The prize is a thousand dollars. If I win, I'll give you the prize money."

"And if you don't win?" asked Mr. Thorndyke.

"If I lose, you can have Herbie," said Jim. "But Herbie and I won't lose."

"We'll see about that," said Mr. Thorndyke. "I shall be in that race, too!"

The El Dorado Road Race was set to begin at ten o'clock in the morning. Jim, Tennessee, and Carole arrived at nine. They did not want Mr. Thorndyke to have any chance to do something to Herbie. Just to make sure, they followed Mr. Thorndyke around for the next hour.

They forgot one thing. Mr. Thorndyke had an assistant—Havershaw!

Fifteen cars were entered in the race. They were lined up in rows on Main Street, which happened to be the only street in El Dorado. Crowds of people had gathered along the sidewalk to watch the start of the race.

The street that led out of the little town quickly turned into a twisting mountain road. That was the course they were to follow until they reached the finish line many miles away.

The race would last for several hours.

At ten o'clock the green flag went up and the race drivers took off. Mr. Thorndyke's car charged ahead but Herbie was right behind it.

Mr. Thorndyke and Havershaw were together in car number fourteen.

"Were you able to do what I told you to do?" asked Mr. Thorndyke.

"Yes, sir," said Havershaw. "I fixed—ha, ha—the little car. It was easy. Douglas and his friends were watching *you* all the time. No one was watching the car."

"Havershaw, you are a real rascal," said Mr. Thorndyke.

"Thank you, sir," said Havershaw.

Twenty minutes later, racing down the mountain road, Mr. Thorndyke was still in the lead. And Jim was still right behind him.

"Havershaw," said Mr. Thorndyke. "Aren't we coming to that dangerous oil spill on the road?"

"I don't see anything, sir," said Havershaw.

"Of course not, you blunderhead!" said Mr. Thorndyke. "Bring out the oil."

"Yes, sir," said Havershaw gleefully.

He grabbed several cans of motor oil from behind his seat. Then he opened a small door in the floorboard of the car and poured the oil onto the road.

Seconds later, Herbie hit the oil spill, skidded off the road, and bounced down the mountainside. Jim, Tennessee, and Carole found themselves going for a very strange and bumpy ride. Herbie seemed to leap over logs and swerve around trees as if he were a jack rabbit. Nothing could stop him. When they came to a pond, Herbie glided across as if it were ice.

At last they could see the road winding below them. A red car was speeding along it.

Inside the red car, Havershaw said, "They're coming down the mountain. We didn't lose them, sir."

"We will, we will," said Mr. Thorndyke. "The sign, please."

"Here you are, sir," said Havershaw as he grabbed a freshly painted board from behind his seat.

At that moment, they came to a fork in the road. A sign there said:

TUNNEL—TURN LEFT
LOST BONANZA MINE—TURN RIGHT

Mr. Thorndyke slammed on the brakes. Havershaw jumped out of the car and hung his sign over the other sign. Now it said:

TUNNEL—TURN RIGHT
LOST BONANZA MINE—TURN LEFT

Meanwhile, Herbie had bounced back onto the road and was racing after the red car. Jim glanced in his rear-view mirror. He saw the other cars coming up behind him.

"We should be coming to a tunnel soon," said Carole, looking at a map.

When they reached the fork in the road, Jim turned right. They found themselves on an old dirt road.

Jim peered ahead. He could see a dark opening in the side of the mountain.

"That must be the tunnel," he said.

Seconds later, Herbie speeded into the Lost Bonanza Mine. As the tunnel grew darker and narrower, Herbie rolled to a stop. Thirteen other race cars stopped behind him.

Jim turned on the headlights and stared ahead. Not far from them was a large box hanging from old rusty chains.

"This isn't a tunnel!" said Jim. "This is a mine. That's a mine elevator up ahead. If we can get Herbie into it, I think we can get out of here."

"But Herbie won't fit," said Tennessee.

"Oh, yes, he will—if we stand him on end," said Jim.

They jumped out. With all three of them pushing, they got Herbie off the ground and up onto his back wheels. Then they rolled him into the elevator. Jim, Tennessee, and Carole squeezed in beside him.

Jim tugged on the chains. Creaking and groaning, the elevator began to rise. Ever so slowly, they moved up the mine shaft. When they reached the top, they were out in the open again. Herbie tumbled out of the elevator and bounced down on all four wheels. Both doors flipped open. Jim and his friends climbed into the little car. Herbie took off.

A mile from the Lost Bonanza Mine, Mr. Thorndyke and Havershaw were sitting under a tree by the side of the road. They were eating a picnic lunch.

"Bring out the champagne," said Mr. Thorndyke. "With all the other cars trapped in that old mine, we can begin to celebrate our victory."

Havershaw took a bottle out of an ice bucket.

"Your champagne, sir," said Havershaw. "It's nicely chilled, the way you like it."

A little white car whizzed by.

"Not now, you idiot!" cried Mr. Thorndyke, dashing for his car. "What do you think this is? A picnic?"

It was not long before Mr. Thorndyke caught up with Jim.

But, try as he would, he could not get past him.

"Havershaw, are you sure you fixed the little car this morning?" asked Mr. Thorndyke.

"Yes, sir," answered Havershaw.

"Then why is it still in one piece?" shrieked Mr. Thorndyke.

Both cars were nearing the finish line. Herbie was still out in front, but Mr. Thorndyke's car was close behind. In less than a minute, one of these two cars would win the race.

Suddenly Jim heard a strange snapping sound. It was coming from below.

"I think we have a problem," called Tennessee from the back seat. "There's a crack in Herbie's floorboard."

Just then Jim heard an odd ripping noise. It was coming from above.

"I think we have another problem," Tennessee called again. "There's a crack in Herbie's roof."

"Is it serious?" asked Jim.

"I think it's serious," said Tennessee. "In fact, I think that Herbie is splitting in two."

At that very moment Herbie came apart. His front half broke away from his back half. Jim and

Carole were left with the steering wheel. Tennessee was left with the engine.

As Jim's half slowed down, Mr. Thorndyke pulled up alongside.

"Too bad!" he shouted, starting to move ahead. "I'll have the pieces sent directly to the auto wreckers."

Mr. Thorndyke had failed to notice something. While he was passing Jim, Tennessee was passing him!

And the next thing they knew, they all rode over the finish line. Tennessee was in the lead. Mr. Thorndyke was next. Jim was last.

That is how Herbie happened to take first and third place in the same race.

Tennessee soon welded Herbie back together again. But, of course, you already guessed *that*.

On the other hand, Mr. Thorndyke soon fell apart. His nerves had been under a terrible strain. He quit the automobile business and began looking for easier work. At last he found something he could do. He went to work in a toothpaste factory. It was his job to put the caps on the tubes of toothpaste.

Left to himself, Havershaw stopped being a rascal. He went on

to win many races, driving Mr. Thorndyke's car.

And what did Jim and Tennessee and Carole do?

They continued to have many wonderful adventures with Herbie. But first, Jim and Tennessee took a long vacation.

It was only a few days after the race that Tennessee came downstairs and found Herbie loaded down with equipment. A beach umbrella was tied to his front end. Two pairs of skis were strapped on at the back. A canoe was nestled on top.

"Shall I bring my swimsuit, my ski pants, or my hiking boots?" Tennessee asked Jim.

"Bring everything," answered. Jim

"Where in the world are we going?" said Tennessee.

"I don't know," said Jim. "I thought we would let Herbie decide!"

How to Make a Love-Bug-Mobile

If you think you're too young to have your own car, you're wrong. If you think a car costs a lot of money, you're wrong again. You can make your own car—or Love-Bug-mobile—for about ten dollars. Here's what you'll have to buy in order to make it:

Four pieces of wood.

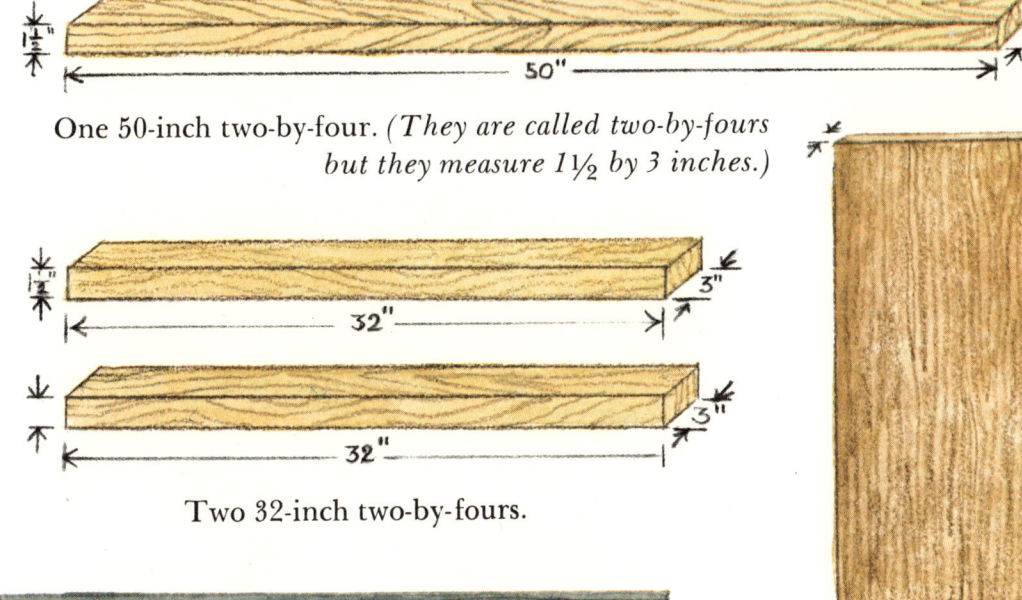

One 50-inch two-by-four. *(They are called two-by-fours but they measure 1½ by 3 inches.)*

Two 32-inch two-by-fours.

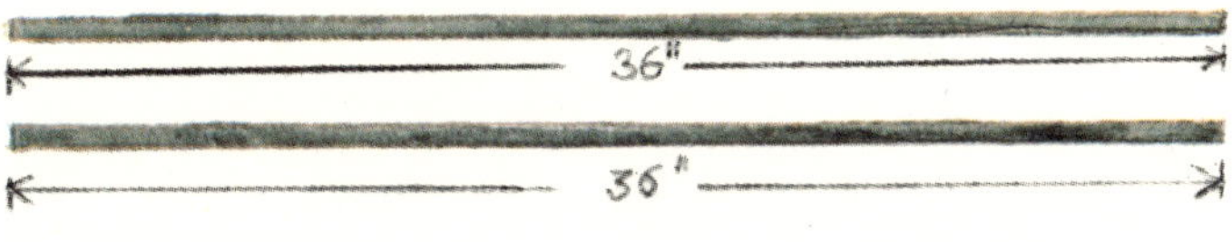

Two ½-inch metal rods 36 inches long.

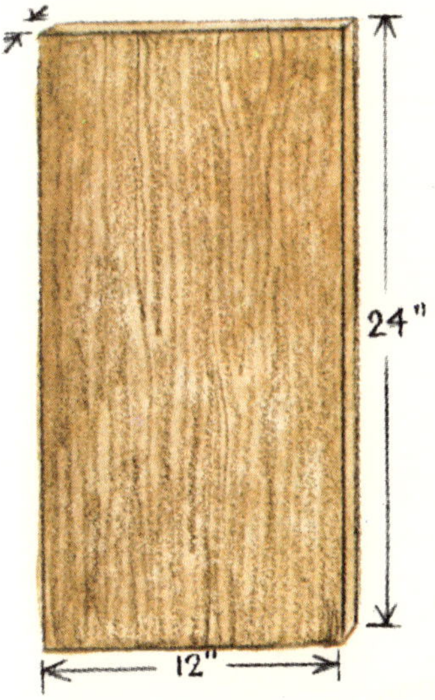

One piece of ¾-inch plywood 24 by 12 inches.

Four ½-inch shaft collars with set screws. *(If you can't find shaft collars, use four axle nuts.)*

Four ¼-inch U-bolts with nuts (¼ by ¾ by 3 inches).

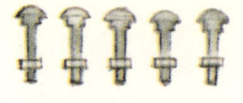
Five ¼-inch countersinking bolts, 3½ inches long, with nuts.

Four washers with ¼-inch centers.

A yardstick.

Two 1-inch-diameter eye screws.

Sandpaper.

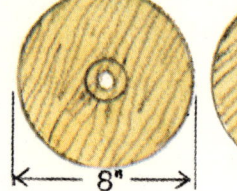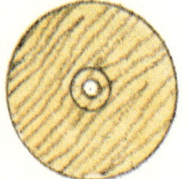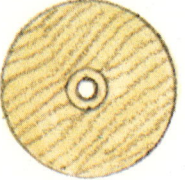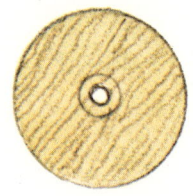
Four 8-inch wagon type wheels.

Six feet of rope. *(Clothesline is good.)*

You can get the wood in a lumberyard. Most hardware stores will have everything else on the list. Bring this book along on your shopping trip so you can show a salesperson exactly what you need. You may want to take along an adult to help carry the materials.

You will also need the following things. If you don't have them around the house you can borrow them from a neighbor.

An eggbeater hand drill with a ¼-inch drill bit.

An adjustable wrench.

A C-clamp.

A sharp pencil with an eraser.

Ask an adult or teen-ager to help you with the building. Here is what the two of you will have to do:

1. Mark the three two-by-fours like this:
  Write **A** on one end and **B** on the other end of the 50-inch board.
  Write **C** and **D** on the ends of one 32-inch board.
  Write **E** and **F** on the ends of the other 32-inch board.

2. On each marked two-by-four draw a line from end to end down the center—1½ inches in from either side.

3. Take two-by-four **AB**. On the center line drill a hole 2 inches from end **A**.

4. On the center line drill a hole 2 inches from end **B**. Then drill another hole 2½ inches from end **B**.

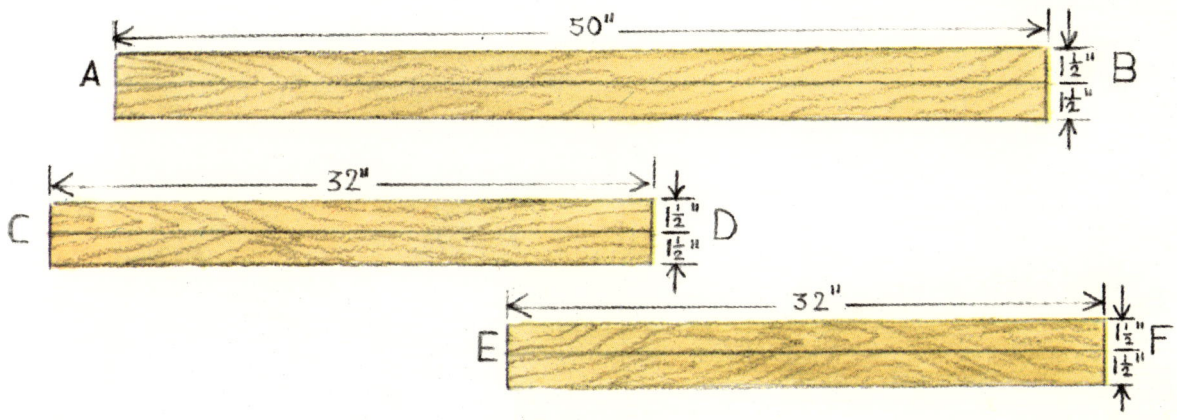

Steps 1 and 2

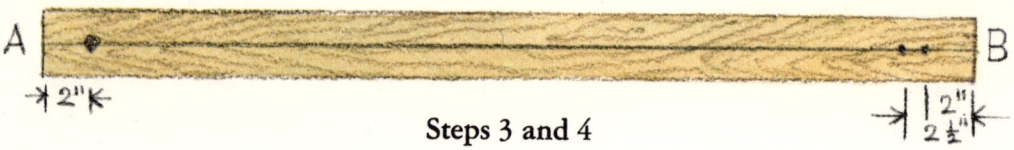

Steps 3 and 4

5. Take the plywood and draw a center line down the 24-inch length —6 inches in from either side.

6. On top of two-by-four **AB** lay the plywood so that one of its ends is 3½ inches from end **B**. The center lines of the plywood and of the two-by-four must match at the ends of the plywood.

7. Clamp the plywood and the two-by-four together with the C-clamp. On the center line, 1 inch in from each end of the plywood, drill a hole through both pieces of wood.

8. Put a countersinking bolt in each of these holes. Hit each bolt with a hammer so it sinks in. Screw a nut on each bolt, and tighten the nut with a wrench. You have now finished the seat of your Love-Bug-mobile.

9. Take two-by-four **CD**. Drill a hole 16 inches from the ends and ½ inch *above* the center line.

10. Put a countersinking bolt in this hole. Hit it with a hammer so it sinks in. **Do not put the nut on yet.**

Step 5

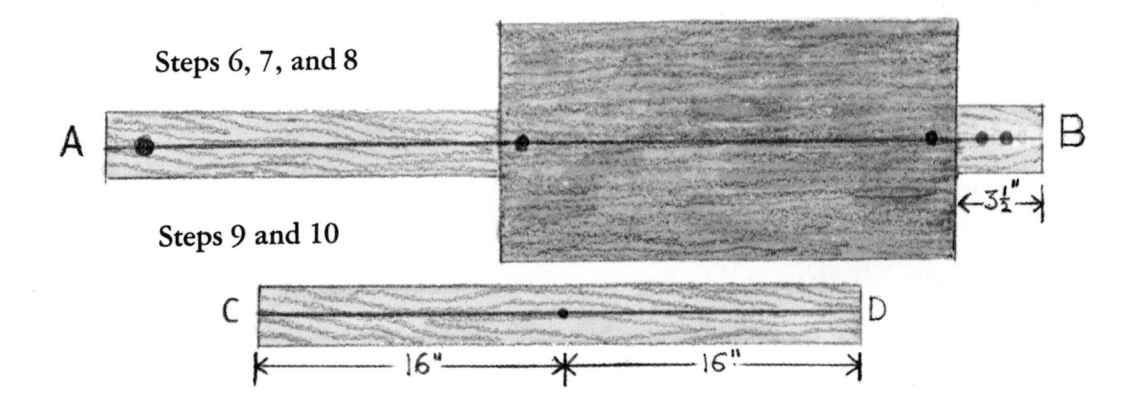

Steps 6, 7, and 8

A ——————————————— B

3½"

Steps 9 and 10

C ——————————————— D

16"   16"

11. Two inches from end **C** first drill a hole ¼ inch above the center line. Then drill a hole ¼ inch below the center line. In the same way, make two more holes 2 inches from end **D**.

12. Take two-by-four **EF**. Two inches from end **E** first drill a hole ¼ inch above the center line. Then drill a hole ¼ inch below the center line. Repeat these two holes 2 inches from end **F**.

13. Sixteen inches from the ends, first drill a hole ¼ inch above the center line. Then drill a hole ¼ inch below the center line.

14. Put a countersinking bolt in each of these center holes. Hit each bolt with a hammer so it sinks in. **Do not put the nut on yet.**

15. Put the U-bolts through the end holes of **CD** and **EF**. Put on the metal plates that come with the U-bolts. Screw on the nuts, **but do not tighten them.**

16. Slide the metal rods through the U-bolts on **CD** and **EF**. Make

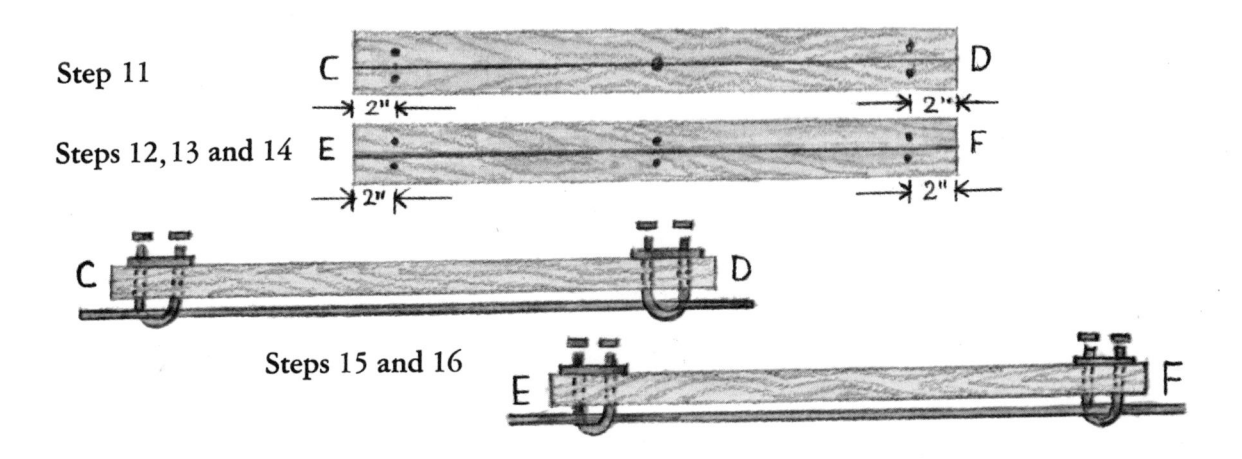

Step 11

C ——————————————— D
2"   2"

Steps 12, 13 and 14

E ——————————————— F
2"   2"

Steps 15 and 16

39

sure that the rods stick out 2 inches past the ends of the wood. Hold the rods in place, and tighten the nuts of the U-bolts.

17. Turn two-by-four **CD** over so the end of the center bolt is sticking up and the rod is under the wood. Put a washer on the center bolt. Turn two-by-four **AB** with the plywood seat face up. Then put the bolt up through the hole at end **A** of two-by-four **AB**.

Steps 17 and 18

18. Put another washer on the end of the bolt, and screw the nut on loosely.

19. Turn two-by-four **EF** over so the center bolts are sticking up. Again, the rod is under the wood. Put the two bolts up through the two holes at end **B** of two-by-four **AB. Do not use any washers between the pieces of wood this time.**

20. Put a washer and nut on each bolt. Tighten **all** the nuts with a wrench.

21. Slide the wheels on the ends of the metal rods. Slide the shaft collars over the ends of the rods and tighten.

22. Put eye screws on the front edge near the ends of two-by-four **CD**. Tie a rope to the screws. **This is your steering rope.**

23. Sand all the rough spots.

How about that! You've built yourself a Love-Bug-mobile. You might want to customize your mobile. You can do that by:

• Adding a back to the seat. (An easy way is to use a beach backrest.)

• Adding a hood and fenders. (Cardboard cartons can be easily cut and shaped.)

Steps 19, 20, 21, and 22

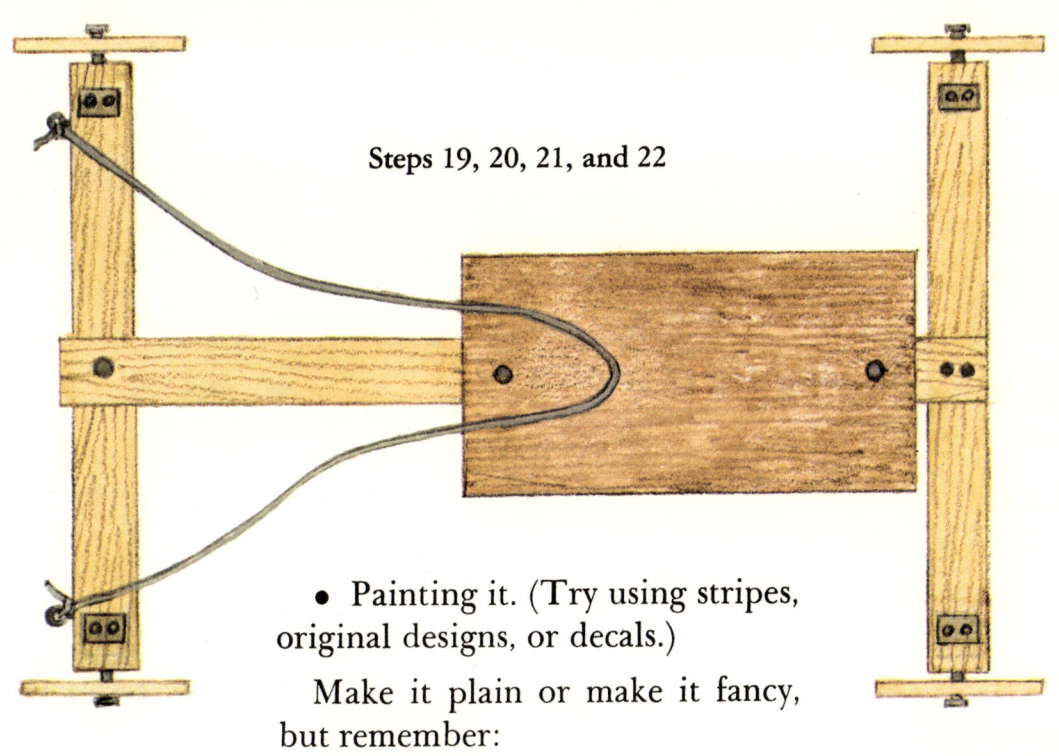

- Painting it. (Try using stripes, original designs, or decals.)

Make it plain or make it fancy, but remember:

KEEP BUGGIN' ALONG!

In Other Words

MANY OF YOU have probably heard these sayings before. But did you know that they have a special meaning on the race track?

JUMP THE GUN   Begin too soon; act hastily

SPIN YOUR WHEELS   Stand still; make no headway

BURN RUBBER   Make a quick start

PIT STOP   A quick stop for repairs, fuel, and refreshment

DEAD HEAT   Finish in a tie

The Indianapolis 500.

U.S. Auto Races

Every year on Memorial Day, at 10:45 A.M., there is a loud boom over the Indianapolis Speedway in Indiana. It is the sound of a giant firecracker called an aerial bomb. Immediately the huge crowd of 300,000 people sends up a great cheer. The aerial bomb is a signal that the Indianapolis 500 will soon begin. And it is a signal for the drivers to line up their cars on the track.

At 11 o'clock another bomb goes off. Now 33 cars are lined up behind the starting line. Three are right at the line. Ten more rows of three are behind them. The cars look like inventions in a science-fiction movie. Each has four fat black tires that seem higher than the body of the car. The front is narrow and sloping. It almost reaches to the ground. In the middle of the car sits the driver in his cockpit. His seat is only inches from the ground. His legs stretch out straight in front of him. Behind the driver is a very powerful engine. And behind the engine is a special tail called an aerofoil tail. It helps the car stay firmly on the ground. But it makes an Indianapolis racer look like an airplane without wings.

A voice calls over the microphone, "Gentlemen, start your engines!" Within a few seconds a deafening roar fills the speedway. Clouds of smoke pour out of the cars and float lazily away.

When the engines are warmed up, the cars start out slowly. They follow a special pace car that leads them around one lap of the track. The cars stay in the positions they have been assigned. But they slowly gain speed as they travel the 2½ miles (about 4 kilometers) back to the starting line. Eighty . . . 90 . . . 100 miles an hour they go.

Around and around they go.

An Indy racer looks like an airplane without wings.

As they pass the starting line, the drivers see a man waving a green flag. The flag is the signal to begin the race. The pace car pulls off the track. The "500" is on! By the time the cars come past the grandstand again, they will be running at 200 miles (320 kilometers) an hour. The first car to go around the track 200 times will win $250,000 for its driver and owners. This prize is the biggest in auto racing.

Racing fans all over the U.S. would love to be at Indianapolis on race day. But they don't have to travel that far to see a car race. Today there are races of many different kinds in all parts of the country that offer the same excitement and drama.

The Daytona 500 is almost as big an event as the Indianapolis 500.

Stock cars.

It is run each February at the Daytona International Speedway in Florida. In many ways this race and the Indianapolis race are similar. They are both run on oval tracks 2½ miles (about 4 kilometers) long. The cars run at about 200 miles (320 kilometers) an hour. And both races are run over a distance of 500 miles (about 800 kilometers). That's why they are called "500s."

But there is one big difference between the two races—the cars. The Daytona 500 is for stock cars. They don't look like wingless airplanes. Instead, they look like the cars people drive every day. But underneath the "stock" body, a stock car is very different from an ordinary passenger car. It has been completely rebuilt with a special racing engine. It also has a stronger frame that includes a "roll bar" above the driver. If the car ever rolls over, the roll bar will keep the roof from being crushed.

Stock car drivers have learned a trick that makes their races very exciting. They found that if a driver can pull his car right behind another car, he has an advantage. He can get pulled along without having to run his engine as hard as the one ahead of him. This is called "drafting." In many races the cars fly around the track at 180

The Daytona 500.

miles (288 kilometers) an hour, only a few feet apart. Sometimes they even bump each other. As the cars round the last curve of the last lap, the second car can suddenly pull out. It can "slingshot" past the leader with a burst of speed to win the race.

A third kind of racing has fans all over the world. It is called road racing because the cars race over a road course. They don't travel around and around an oval as at Indianapolis or Daytona. Instead, they race on a course that has sharp turns, hills, and sometimes even mountains.

The early road courses were ordinary roads that wound through the countryside and even through towns. In one race in Europe, the course came down a steep hill. Then it made a sudden turn just as the road seemed about to go into the sea. One driver's brakes failed

A road racer.

Grand Prix—Spain.

Grand Prix—Watkins Glen.

on the hill, and he went right into the ocean. (He was fished out unhurt.)

Today the most famous road races are those in the Grand Prix series. ("*Grand Prix*" is grand prize in French.) Each race in the series is run in a different country—some in Europe and some in North America. The cars are a lot like those that race at Indianapolis. Their engines are behind the driver, and they have aerofoil tails.

The United States Grand Prix is run each year in early October. It is held at a special road course in Watkins Glen, New York. Like Indianapolis and Daytona, the Watkins Glen race attracts a huge crowd. Thousands want to watch the world's most skilled drivers. The fans line up along the course, which winds through woods and fields. They watch their favorites skid around the sudden corners, speed up on the straight sections, and keep ahead of the other drivers. The driver who wins the most Grand Prix races in a year is named the world champion driver.

Racing is a dangerous sport. Many drivers have been killed in crashes and others have been badly injured. Racing fans know this. But they also know that auto racing is one of the most spectacular and exciting sports ever invented.

Soap Box Derby

Some people call it the Gravity Grand Prix. Others call it the All American Downhill Derby. But it doesn't make a great deal of difference what you call it. Anyone who has watched or been in a soap box derby will tell you it's a great sport.

Many years ago, stores got soap in wooden boxes or crates. It didn't take long for somebody to think about putting four wheels and a steering control on the empty soap crates. And there it was, a soap box car.

No one knows exactly when the soap box races started. Probably they began when some young driver challenged another to a race—downhill, of course.

From this small start, soap box racing grew. Adults began to take an interest in the competition. Someone thought of building a special track, *off* city streets so an accident wouldn't spoil the fun. Other people suggested rules about car sizes and weight. They wanted to keep the competition fair for everyone. Today any driver between the ages of 10 and 15 can enter.

One derby rule is that the driver of a car must also be the builder. Building your own car is something special. If the car goes fast and is easy to control, you can be proud, especially if you win. Of course, if the car is hard to control or can't get up speed, then you know where to put the blame.

The officials who run today's soap box derby races don't want young racers to spend a lot of money on a car. So the rules say you can spend only a certain amount, usually less than 50 dollars. To many people, 50 dollars is a lot of money. That's why derby officials sometimes find adults to help young people raise the money.

When you build your own car you follow a rule book. The rules tell how to put a *skid* or *drag* brake, steering control, and axles in the car. The rules also tell you how long, wide, and heavy your car can be. Other rules keep people from putting special parts in their cars to make them go extra fast.

While you build and test your car, you can use any soap box derby wheels. But these are only for testing and practice. On race day, the practice wheels come off your car. You get a new set of wheels, exactly matched to the wheels the other racers must use.

Since the derby is a downhill race, there are no engines or fuels. But the cars have to be built with very good steering control. Many cars go faster than 35 miles (56 kilometers) per hour on the downhill run. If a car spins off the track at that speed, the car, the driver, and even the spectators can be in danger.

Building a real soap box racer is not easy. The rules say the driver-builder can have a *little* help from an adult. But not much. Before the race, derby officials ask you ques-

The derby may mean new friends.

A clinic is serious business.

tions about your car. They can tell from your answers if you really built the car yourself or just helped someone else build it for you.

How do you get into soap box racing? In many cities and towns people in groups or clubs sponsor the events. Some of these groups might be the Elks, Kiwanis, Rotary, or Junior Chamber of Commerce. You can get help finding a soap box sponsor by writing to the General Manager, All American Soap Box Derby, 789 Derby Downs Drive, Akron, Ohio 44306.

If you decide to enter soap box races, your work begins around February. At a meeting you sign up for the races. You get a rule book, plans for building a car, and a chance to see some derby cars. And you meet other people who want to race. Between February and April you have time to build your car. While you're doing the work, you can take your unfinished car to a meeting called a *clinic*. Officials at the clinic look at your car. They tell you if you're following the rules, and they answer your questions.

At a clinic you learn the names of tools and how to use them. You also meet other people who are building cars. These people may become your friends. But when it's race time, these friends will be your competitors!

Around the beginning of April, your work is finished and it's time to practice. Now you find out if you built your car according to the rules. The derby officials want you to have time to make changes before the big races. The officials check your brakes and the size of your car. They also weigh it with you in it. If you and your car together weigh more than 250 pounds (about 112 kilograms), you have to take some weight off your car—or yourself. If you and your car weigh in under 250 pounds, you can either add weight to your car, or start eating lots of bananas and potatoes.

When you first try your car on the soap box track, the course may look a little scary. You will be in a starting gate. A metal arm holds your car in place. In front of you is the steep, 1,000-foot-long (1,600-meter-long) downhill track. The beginning of the track is steepest. This makes the car accelerate. The track is not as steep at the end.

You're in the gate. An official asks, "Are you ready?"

You answer, "Yes." The arm drops. Your car is out of the gate and gaining speed. Now you know why the rules are so strict. The wind whistling around your helmet lets you know why you need good steering control and good brakes.

On race day you go through one more inspection. There's still time to add weight—pieces of metal—if

It's a steep track!

The gate is down. The race is on!

your car needs it. Or maybe you should stop drinking water if the scale goes *over* 250 pounds. Once you have weighed in, you draw a number. It tells what racing lane you'll have on the track.

For each race in the event, you go into the gate with two other competitors. No more practice. This is it, the real race! The metal arm drops. Three cars streak toward the finish line and an automatic camera takes a picture of the finish. The picture shows which car crossed the finish line first, and an official declares the winner.

If you're a good driver and have built a good car, you have a chance to win. Winners in each race go on to race against other winners. Each heat gets faster because the losers are no longer in the competition. The winner of the last race is declared the champion of the event. A local event champion may go into statewide races. Winners of statewide races go into the National Championship at Akron, Ohio, where the prizes are big.

But derby people say championships are not everything. People who enter the soap box derby gain something even if they don't win. They learn about tools and car parts and have a chance to build a beautiful car. They win new friends. And they learn how it feels to do their best in competition. Maybe it's true when people say, "There are more winners than losers in soap box racing."

Goofy Enters The Soap Box Derby

THE DAY WAS BRIGHT. The sun was bright. Everything was bright except Goofy.

"What's a soap box derby?" he asked. "Something to wear on your head?"

"It's a race for cars built out of soap boxes," said Mickey. "They just *call* it a derby."

Goofy went on reading the sign: "Saturday, April eighth! . . . G-a-w-r-s-h, Mickey! That's *tomorrow!* It hardly gives me any time at all."

"You're not thinking of building a racer and entering the derby, are you, Goofy?"

"I sure would like to." Goofy looked sad. "But I don't have a soap box."

"You don't need a soap box. You can use any kind of box. In fact, you can build your racer out of almost anything!"

"Gee whiz! Then I'm going home to start building one right away! See you tomorrow, Mickey!"

"Good luck!" called Mickey.

On the way home, Goofy began to think about what he would need to build his racer. The most important thing, he decided, was wheels . . . four of them. Now where could he get four wheels in a hurry?

Maybe that lady coming down the street would sell him the wheels off her baby carriage. Certainly no harm in asking. Goofy lifted his hat politely as the lady came closer.

"Pardon me, lady," Goofy began. "You wouldn't want to sell your baby—"

BOP! Before poor Goofy could say "carriage," the lady had whacked him over the head with her pocketbook. The next thing he knew he was sitting on the sidewalk, rubbing his head. The lady and her baby carriage were zooming away down Main Street.

54

Goofy decided to try BLOTKIN'S HARDWARE STORE *They* should have all kinds of wheels!

"Can you sell me four wheels?" he asked the man in the store.

"What kind of wheels?"

Goofy thought for a minute. "Round ones! I need them right away to build a racer for the soap box derby."

This guy must be some kind of a nut, Mr. Blotkin thought. But a sale is a sale.

"How about a nice wheelbarrow?" Mr. Blotkin suggested, pointing to one of his most expensive models.

"But it's only got one wheel!" Goofy protested.

"No problem!" Mr. Blotkin replied. "I'll be glad to sell you *four* wheelbarrows!"

"Gee, that's a good idea!" said Goofy. "You sure are smart, Mr. Blotkin."

thought so, because that's exactly what it was.

The first person Goofy showed his racer to was Mickey. Mickey always appreciated his genius.

All night long Goofy hammered and sawed, and sawed and hammered. By the morning, he had his soap box racer all ready for the big day. Of course *some* people might have thought the racer looked like a wheelbarrow with four wheels. In fact, *most* people would have

56

"Tell me the truth, Mickey. . . . Did you ever see anything like this?" Goofy asked proudly.

"No. I can honestly say I never have!" answered Mickey, looking at the strange machine and scratching his head. "What is it?"

Well, maybe Mickey *didn't* always appreciate his genius!

"It's my soap box derby car! That's what it is!"

"You mean you're going down Ferguson Hill in *that*?" Mickey gulped.

"You just watch me!" Goofy cried.

"I wouldn't miss it for the world!" said Mickey.

Ferguson Hill was a bustling beehive of activity when Goofy and Mickey arrived on the scene.

"Looks as if the races have already started!" Goofy observed, as three soap box racers sped by on the downhill track.

He pulled his car up to a man who stood at the top of the crowded hill. "Can you tell me where to find an official?" Goofy asked.

make your car."

Goofy tugged his wheelbarrow racer up to the starting line.

"Look, Mickey! Everybody is staring at my racer!" Goofy beamed with pride and delight.

"I can't imagine why!" answered Mickey.

Goofy found a place between two other racers at the starting line. Suddenly, from the sidelines, Mickey stared at Goofy's racer with horror. Something important was missing! But it was too late now...

The official's voice called out: "READY...GET SET...GO!"

"What do you think *I* am, sonny?" the official answered.

"Beats me," said Goofy. "All I know is I want to enter this race."

"Forget it, pal. Your car doesn't meet our rules."

"But I spent all night building this car. You've *got* to let me race."

"Well..." the official wavered. "I guess maybe we could let you enter the race this time, but next time, read the rules before you

The racers took off down Ferguson Hill.

As Goofy's wheelbarrow racer rolled away from the starting line, it began to pick up speed. Faster and faster it rumbled down the steep hill.

Just before the car veered off the track, Goofy discovered what was missing. He had forgotten to put a steering wheel on his car! The racer cut a path through a crowd of people.

Goofy shut his eyes and clung tightly to the sides of the wheelbarrow as his racer zoomed straight for a cement wall.

Goofy and his racer cleared the wall, but then a tree got in their way.

The next thing Goofy knew, he was sitting in the shade of a very sturdy oak tree.

"Goofy! Are you all right?" It was his friend Mickey, kneeling anxiously beside him.

"I guess so! A couple of loose teeth maybe... What happened?"

"You hit that tree!" Mickey said. "I hope you learned a lesson from all this, Goofy!"

Goofy nodded.

"I sure did! Next year I'm gonna buy five wheelbarrows and make a steering wheel!"